4Ominute
BIBLE STUDIES

The Essentials of Effective Prayer

Kay Arthur, David & BJ Lawson

PRECEPT MINISTRIES INTERNATIONAL

WATERBROOK
PRESS

THE ESSENTIALS OF EFFECTIVE PRAYER
PUBLISHED BY WATERBROOK PRESS
12265 Oracle Boulevard, Suite 200
Colorado Springs, Colorado 80921

All Scripture quotations are taken from the New American Standard Bible®. © Copyright
The Lockman Foundation 1960, 1962, 1963, 1968, 1971, 1972, 1973, 1975, 1977, 1995.
Used by permission. (www.Lockman.org).

ISBN 978-0-307-45770-7

Published in the United States by WaterBrook Multnomah, an imprint of the Crown
Publishing Group, a division of Random House Inc., New York.

WATERBROOK and its deer colophon are registered trademarks of Random House Inc.

Printed in the United States of America
2014

10 9 8

SPECIAL SALES
Most WaterBrook Multnomah books are available at special quantity discounts when
purchased in bulk by corporations, organizations, and special-interest groups. Custom
imprinting or excerpting can also be done to fit special needs. For information, please
e-mail SpecialMarkets@WaterBrookMultnomah.com or call 1-800-603-7051.

HOW TO USE THIS STUDY

This small-group study is for people who are interested in learning for themselves more about what the Bible says on various subjects, but who have only limited time to meet together. It's ideal, for example, for a lunch group at work, an early morning men's group, a young mothers' group meeting in a home, a Sunday-school class, or even family devotions. (It's also ideal for small groups that typically have longer meeting times—such as evening groups or Saturday morning groups—but want to devote only a portion of their time together to actual study, while reserving the rest for prayer, fellowship, or other activities.)

This book is designed so that all the group's participants will complete each lesson's study activities *at the same time.* Discussing your insights drawn from what God says about the subject reveals exciting, life-impacting truths.

Although it's a group study, you'll need a facilitator to lead the study and keep the discussion moving. (This person's function is *not* that of a lecturer or teacher. However, when this book is used in a Sunday-school class or similar setting, the teacher should feel free to lead more directly and to bring in other insights in addition to those provided in each week's lesson.)

If *you* are your group's facilitator, the leader, here are some helpful points for making your job easier:

- Go through the lesson and mark the text before you lead the group. This will give you increased familiarity with the material and will enable you to facilitate the group with greater ease. It may be easier for you to lead the group through the instructions for marking if you, as a leader, choose a specific color for each symbol you mark.

- As you lead the group, start at the beginning of the text and simply read it aloud in the order it appears in the lesson, including the "insight boxes," which appear throughout. Work through the lesson together, observing and discussing what you learn. As you read the Scripture verses, have the group say aloud the word they are marking in the text.

- The discussion questions are there simply to help you cover the material. As the class moves into the discussion, many times you will find that they will cover the questions on their own. Remember, the discussion questions are there to guide the group through the topic, not to squelch discussion.

- Remember how important it is for people to verbalize their answers and discoveries. This greatly strengthens their personal understanding of each week's lesson. Try to ensure that everyone has plenty of opportunity to contribute to each week's discussions.

- Keep the discussion moving. This may mean spending more time on some parts of the study than on others. If necessary, you should feel free to spread out a lesson over more than one session. However, remember that you don't want to slow the pace too much. It's much better to leave everyone "wanting more" than to have people dropping out because of declining interest.

- If the validity or accuracy of some of the answers seems questionable, you can gently and cheerfully remind the group to stay focused on the truth of the Scriptures. Your object is to learn what the Bible says, not to engage in human philosophy. Simply stick with the Scriptures and give God the opportunity to speak. His Word *is* truth (John 17:17)!

THE ESSENTIALS OF EFFECTIVE PRAYER

Do you pray?

Really, do you pray? How often? How effective do your prayers seem to be?

Do you question whether your prayer life is all it should be? Do you ever wonder if God still answers when people pray? Do you worry that you don't truly understand what prayer really is?

If you've asked yourself these questions, you are not alone. Almost all of us have questioned at some time what prayer really is and how—or if—it really works.

In this study we will discover the answers to these questions as we examine what Scripture teaches about prayer and consider how to apply those truths to our own lives.

We also will explore the connection between prayer and pleasing God. A. W. Tozer, a man known for the vitality of his prayer life, once wrote, "What the praying man does is to bring his will into line with the will of God so God can do what He has all along been willing to do."[1]

For the next six weeks we will learn how to bring our will in line with the will of God. We hope that by the end of this study your prayer life will be more exciting and vibrant than ever before.

---

[1] A. W. Tozer, *The Price of Neglect*, comp. Harry Verploegh (Camp Hill, PA: Christian Publications, 1991), 51–52.

We know prayer has to do with communicating with God, but what exactly does that look like? What's the point of praying? Does a sovereign God really care about our concerns? And if He does, how should we approach Him? What sort of things do we ask for or talk to Him about?

This week we'll try to understand the nature and purpose of prayer by examining some people of prayer and references to prayer in the Bible.

OBSERVE

James, the brother of Jesus, in his New Testament letter mentioned one of the great men of prayer from the Old Testament: Elijah.

Leader: Read James 5:16b–18.
  • *Have the group say aloud and mark the words **prayer** and **prayed** with a **P**.*

As you read the text, it's helpful to have the group say the key words aloud as they mark them. This way everyone will be sure they are marking every occurrence of the word, including any synonymous words or phrases. Do this throughout the study.

JAMES 5:16B–18

16 The effective prayer of a righteous man can accomplish much.

17 Elijah was a man with a nature like ours, and he prayed earnestly that it would not rain, and it did not rain on the earth for three years and six months.

18 Then he prayed again, and the sky poured rain and the earth produced its fruit.

DISCUSS

• What did you learn from marking the references to *prayer* in this passage?

• Have you ever had an experience like Elijah's? Do you feel that your prayers "accomplish much"? Explain your answer.

• Elijah was a man like us, but his prayer life was unlike most of ours. It is a little intimidating, isn't it? Over the next six weeks we will see what it takes to transform our prayer life into one like Elijah's.

1 KINGS 8:27–30, 38–39

27 "But will God indeed dwell on the earth? Behold, heaven and the highest heaven cannot contain You, how much less this house which I have built!

OBSERVE

Let's look at a prayer offered by King Solomon, the third king of ancient Israel, at the dedication of the first temple of God in Jerusalem.

Leader: *Read 1 Kings 8:27–30, 38–39. Have the group say aloud and...*

• *put an* **S** *over each reference to* **Solomon.** *Since he is speaking in this passage, watch carefully for pronouns and synonyms that refer to him, including the phrase* **Your servant.**

• *mark every reference to* **prayer** *with a* **P,** *including synonyms such as* **supplication, cry,** *and* **spreading his hands.**

INSIGHT

Supplication in this passage refers to a request for favor or grace.

DISCUSS

• What did you learn from marking the references to *Solomon?*

• What did you learn from marking the references to *prayer* in this passage?

28 "Yet have regard to the prayer of Your servant and to his supplication, O LORD my God, to listen to the cry and to the prayer which Your servant prays before You today;

29 that Your eyes may be open toward this house night and day, toward the place of which You have said, 'My name shall be there,' to listen to the prayer which Your servant shall pray toward this place.

30 "Listen to the supplication of Your servant and of Your people Israel, when they pray toward this place; hear in heaven Your dwelling place; hear and forgive.

38 whatever prayer or supplication is made by any man or by all Your people Israel, each knowing the affliction of his own heart, and spreading his hands toward this house;

39 then hear in heaven Your dwelling place, and forgive and act and render to each according to all his ways, whose heart You know, for You alone know the hearts of all the sons of men."

• How did Solomon characterize God's relationship with His people?

• What was he asking of God?

• Discuss the synonyms for prayer that you marked in this passage. What do they reveal about the nature of prayer?

OBSERVE

The book of Psalms is a collection of songs and prayers for the people of God. We will look at three psalms of David. The first was written when he fled from Absalom, his son who led a conspiracy to take not only David's throne but also his life (2 Samuel 15).

Leader: Read Psalm 3:1–5 aloud. Have the group...

- *put a* **D** *over each occurrence of the pronouns **my, me, him,** and **I** when they refer to **David,** who is speaking in this passage.*
- *put a* **P** *over the phrase **crying to the Lord.***

INSIGHT

The word *selah* appears frequently in the psalms. Its meaning is unclear, but many scholars believe *selah* is a musical term indicating a pause in the music.

DISCUSS

- What did you learn about David in verses 1 and 2? How would you describe his emotions at this point?

- The word *but* in verse 3 signals a contrast, a change in direction. According to verses 4 and 5, what actions did David take in the

PSALM 3:1–5

1 O LORD, how my adversaries have increased! Many are rising up against me.

2 Many are saying of my soul, "There is no deliverance for him in God." Selah.

3 But You, O LORD, are a shield about me, My glory, and the One who lifts my head.

4 I was crying to the LORD with my voice, And He answered me from His holy mountain. Selah.

5 I lay down and slept; I awoke, for the LORD sustains me.

midst of his enemies and their taunting, and why did he pursue this course of action?

• What phrase is used in this passage to describe prayer?

• When God answered David's prayer, how did David respond? What shift does this indicate from the emotions he felt at the start of the prayer?

• Think of a time you felt worried or oppressed, when it seemed all the odds were against you. What did you do?

Leader: *Invite someone in the group to share such a situation from their personal experience and describe how they responded.*

• Discuss what you've learned about prayer from this passage and how you can apply it to your life.

OBSERVE

Leader: Read aloud Psalm 4:1–5. Have the group…

- *put a **P** over every reference to **prayer**, including the phrases **when I call** and **meditate in your heart**.*
- *mark every reference to **God**, including pronouns and synonyms, with a triangle: △*

DISCUSS

- Once again David was clearly in a stressful situation. How did he respond?

- What did he expect God to do in regard to his prayer? On what did David base his expectation?

- What did you learn about God from this passage?

- What did you observe about our emotions in connection with prayer, according

PSALM 4:1–5

1 Answer me [David] when I call, O God of my righteousness! You have relieved me in my distress; be gracious to me and hear my prayer.

2 O sons of men, how long will my honor become a reproach? How long will you love what is worthless and aim at deception? Selah.

3 But know that the LORD has set apart the godly man for Himself; the LORD hears when I call to Him.

4 Tremble, and do not sin; meditate in your heart upon your bed, and be still. Selah.

5 Offer the sacrifices of righteousness, and trust in the LORD.

to verses 4 and 5? What choice do we have other than denying our emotions or giving in to them? Explain your answer.

• How can you apply what you have just learned about prayer the next time you encounter a stressful situation?

PSALM 5:1–3

1 Give ear to my words, O LORD, consider my groaning.

2 Heed the sound of my cry for help, my King and my God, for to You I pray.

3 In the morning, O LORD, You will hear my voice; in the morning I will order my prayer to You and eagerly watch.

OBSERVE

We've seen that when David encountered stressful situations, rather than giving in to his fears or focusing on his circumstances, he called out to God and trusted in Him. The result was peace in the midst of the difficulty as David offered up a sacrifice of righteousness. Now let's look at one more example from this man of prayer.

Leader: Read Psalm 5:1–3 aloud. Have the group...

• *put a* **D** *over each occurrence of the pronouns* **my** *and* **I,** *which refer to* **David,** *who is speaking in this passage.*

• *put a* **P** *over every reference to* **prayer,** *including synonyms such as* **my words, my groaning,** *and* **my cry.**

DISCUSS

• Discuss what you learned about David and his character from this passage. What were his first thoughts each day?

• What did you learn from marking the references to *prayer?* What was David praying for, and what did he expect to happen?

Leader: If time permits, invite someone to share with the group how they plan to apply the teachings of this passage to their own life.

OBSERVE

So far we've seen prayer described as crying out to God. Crying out in pain, in fear, in desperation. Most of us can identify with that kind of prayer. But prayer isn't limited to crying out for help in times of trouble; it can serve an even greater purpose, as we'll see in the next few passages.

First, let's look at some verses from Isaiah, in which God describes what's wrong with the prayers of the people of Jerusalem. Although this is a negative example, it serves to teach us another way to describe what prayer is really about.

ISAIAH 29:13–14

13 Then the Lord said, "Because this people draw near with their words and honor Me with their lip service, but they remove their hearts far from Me, and their reverence for Me consists of tradition learned by rote,

14 therefore behold, I will once again deal marvelously with this people, wondrously marvelous; and the wisdom of their wise men will perish, and the discernment of their discerning men will be concealed."

Leader: *Read Isaiah 29:13–14 aloud. Have the group…*
  - *circle every reference to **the people,** including pronouns.*
  - *put a **P** over the phrases **draw near** and **honor me.***

DISCUSS

- What did you learn from marking the references to *the people* in the passage?

- How did the people draw near to God? Were their hearts in it? Explain your answer.

- In this context what does *draw near* mean?

- How did God feel about the people drawing near?

- What was His response?

- Would God answer their prayers? Why or why not?

- Discuss how this passage might be relevant to our worship services and prayer life today.

OBSERVE

Leader: Read Hebrews 4:14–16; 7:25; and 10:19–22 aloud. Have the group say and...
  - *circle each occurrence of the pronouns **we, us,** and **our,** which refer to believers.*
  - *mark each reference to **Jesus,** including pronouns such as **He** and **Him** and synonyms such as **high priest** and **One,** with a cross:* ✝
  - *put a **P** over the phrase **draw near.***

DISCUSS

- What did you learn from marking the references to *believers* in these verses? What do we have, and what are we to do?

HEBREWS 4:14–16

14 Therefore, since we have a great high priest who has passed through the heavens, Jesus the Son of God, let us hold fast our confession.

15 For we do not have a high priest who cannot sympathize with our weaknesses, but One who has been tempted in all things as we are, yet without sin.

16 Therefore let us draw near with confidence to the throne of grace, so that we may receive mercy and find grace to help in time of need.

• For what purpose(s) would we draw near to the throne of God?

HEBREWS 7:25

25 Therefore He is able also to save forever those who draw near to God through Him, since He always lives to make intercession for them.

• What gives us the confidence to approach Him?

HEBREWS 10:19–22

19 Therefore, brethren, since we have confidence to enter the holy place by the blood of Jesus,

• What did you learn about prayer from these verses?

20 by a new and living way which He inaugurated for us through the veil, that is, His flesh,

• Discuss what we can expect when we pray and how this applies to your own prayer life.

21 and since we have a great priest over the house of God,

22 let us draw near with a sincere heart in full assurance of faith, having our hearts sprinkled clean from an evil conscience and our bodies washed with pure water.

WRAP IT UP

Have you listened to others pray and felt intimidated because their words sounded so well composed? Relax. Prayer doesn't require an appointment, it doesn't require proper attire, and it doesn't even require proper grammar. As David's example shows, prayer is as natural as crying out. Crying out and telling God what is on your heart. Crying out and telling God what you need. Crying out and making supplication.

What is prayer? Prayer is simply drawing near to God and talking with Him. As we read in Hebrews 4, we have access to Him through our high priest, Jesus Christ. Because of Him, we can enter the throne room of heaven and draw near to God. There we can cry out, we can ask for help, we can lay our troubles at His feet. Then, as David demonstrated in psalms 3 and 4, we can rest because we know the Lord sustains us.

This week set aside some time to cry out to God about the concerns of your heart. Draw near to Him and enjoy His presence.

Leader: If you have time, pause for the group to pray silently. Encourage them to cry out to God about the concerns of their hearts. Encourage them to draw near to Him and enjoy His presence. After a few minutes of silence, close in prayer, asking God to teach your group to pray.

We saw last week that prayer can be defined as "drawing near to God." In prayer we can be honest about our concerns and entrust them to God. As reassuring as that is, it brings up some new questions: if prayer is that simple, why do so many of us have weak prayer lives? Is it possible for an "ordinary" Christian to pray with the passion of David and the power of Elijah? This week we will begin to answer those questions.

OBSERVE

Prayer, conversation with His Father, was a hallmark of Jesus' life on earth, a fact that didn't escape the disciples' notice.

Leader: Read Luke 11:1 aloud.
 • *Have the group say aloud and mark the words **praying** and **pray** with a **P.***

LUKE 11:1

¹ It happened that while Jesus was praying in a certain place, after He had finished, one of His disciples said to Him, "Lord, teach us to pray just as John also taught his disciples."

— place, away from people.
— teach us. —they went to him.
'taught' — requires learning.

DISCUSS

 • What did you learn from marking *praying* and *pray*?

 • Have you ever been intimidated by the prayer life of someone else, perhaps thinking, *I could never pray like that*? Relate your experience to how the disciples might have felt after hearing Jesus pray.

- they had the desire + humility to ask + learn.

• What request did the disciples make, and what does it show us about their heart?

• What about you? Do you have a heart to learn how to pray? The desire to pray is the most important element in learning how.

MATTHEW 6:5–8

5 "When you pray, you are not to be like the hypocrites; for they love to stand and pray in the synagogues and on the street corners so that they may be seen by men. Truly I say to you, they have their reward in full.

6 "But you, when you pray, go into your inner room, close your door and pray to your Father who is in secret, and your Father

OBSERVE

In Matthew 6, part of the Sermon on the Mount, we find Jesus' classic teaching on prayer. His instructions here will form our outline for the next few weeks as we learn how we are to pray.

Leader: Read Matthew 6:5–8 aloud. Have the group ...
  • *underline each occurrence of the phrase* **when you.**
  • *mark each occurrence of the words* **pray** *and* **praying** *with a* **P.**

DISCUSS

• From what you read in this passage, did Jesus expect His followers to pray? Explain your answer. *yes.*

- What else did you learn from marking the references to praying? What two things are we not to do when praying?

- Was Jesus forbidding public prayer? Explain your answer.

- What do you think Jesus meant by "meaningless repetition"?

- How can we identify and avoid meaningless repetition in our prayers today?

OBSERVE

Let's look next at what is often called the Lord's Prayer, which many students of Scripture view as a model for prayer.

Leader: Read Matthew 6:9–13 aloud. Have the group say and...
- *put a **P** over the word **pray.***
- *mark every reference to **God,** including pronouns such as **Your** and the synonym **Father,** with a triangle:* △

MATTHEW 6:9–13

who sees what is done in secret will reward you.

7 "And when you are praying, do not use meaningless repetition as the Gentiles do, for they suppose that they will be heard for their many words.

8 "So do not be like them; for your Father knows what you need before you ask Him."

9 "Pray, then, in this way: 'Our Father who is in heaven, hallowed be Your name.

10 'Your kingdom come. Your will be done, on earth as it is in heaven.

11 'Give us this day our daily bread.

12 'And forgive us our debts, as we also have forgiven our debtors.

13 'And do not lead us into temptation, but deliver us from evil. [For Yours is the kingdom and the power and the glory forever. Amen.]' "

DISCUSS

• In light of what we read earlier in Matthew 6:7, do Jesus' words in verse 9 indicate that He intended His disciples to repeat these exact words on a regular basis? Explain your answer.

• If the Lord's Prayer provides a basic structure for our conversations with God, we should note the key elements it suggests. Read through the passage again, watching for these elements, and next to each key element listed below, note the verse number(s) where it appears.

<u>9, 13</u>   Worship—showing reverence

<u>10</u>   Declaration of allegiance—stating where your loyalties lie

<u>11</u>   Petition—making a request

<u>12</u>   Confession of sin—seeking forgiveness

<u>13</u>   Request for deliverance—pleading for protection

• What element begins and ends this prayer? What does this suggest?

WORSHIP - Show reverence

• Discuss what you've observed so far about the Lord's Prayer and how it will impact your prayer life.

OBSERVE

We've seen that Jesus gave His disciples a model for prayer that began and ended with worship, with acknowledging God in heaven and exalting His name. Let's see what we can learn from others who incorporated worship in their prayers, starting with Jehoshaphat, an ancient Jewish king from the line of David and Solomon.

Leader: Read aloud 2 Chronicles 20:1–4. Have the group...
- *put a **J** over every reference to **Jehoshaphat**, including pronouns.*
- *put a **P** over each occurrence of the phrases **seek the Lord** and **seek help from the Lord.***

DISCUSS

• What do verses 1 and 2 reveal about Jehoshaphat's situation?

2 CHRONICLES 20:1–4

1 Now it came about after this that the sons of Moab and the sons of Ammon, together with some of the Meunites, came to make war against Jehoshaphat.

2 Then some came and reported to Jehoshaphat, saying, "A great multitude is coming against you from beyond the sea, out of Aram and behold, they are in Hazazon-tamar (that is Engedi)."

³ Jehoshaphat was afraid and turned his attention to seek the LORD, and proclaimed a fast throughout all Judah.

⁴ So Judah gathered together to seek help from the LORD; they even came from all the cities of Judah to seek the LORD.

• What was his initial response? How did he overcome it? *fear — he turned to the Lord*

• What did Jehoshaphat lead Judah to do and why? *FAST → seek the LORD*

• Discuss how this course of action would apply to our lives today. *Pray about our big problems*

---

2 CHRONICLES 20:5–12

⁵ Then Jehoshaphat stood in the assembly of Judah and Jerusalem, in the house of the LORD before the new court,

⁶ and he said, "O LORD, the God of our fathers, are You not God in the heavens? And are You not ruler over all the kingdoms

OBSERVE

Jehoshaphat and his people faced a grave threat, so the king turned to the Lord. As you read his prayer in this next passage, watch carefully to see how he incorporates the element of worship.

Leader: Read 2 Chronicles 20:5–12 aloud. Have the group...
- *mark every reference to **God**, including synonyms and pronouns, with a triangle as before.*
- *put a **P** over the word **cry**.*

DISCUSS

- Briefly summarize Jehoshaphat's description of God. *Ruler, Powerful, friend of Abraham,*

- Compare Jehoshaphat's prayer with the Lord's Prayer. What similarities do you notice? *Worship, Honor*

- What did Jehoshaphat remind God about in verses 7–9? *God gave them this land. And reminded that Sanctuary + that He will deliver them*

- In which verse do you find Jehoshaphat's request, or petition, to God? What, specifically, did he ask for?
  - deliverance.
  - judgement upon them.
  Not particularly specific
  Asks God to be God.

of the nations? Power and might are in Your hand so that no one can stand against You.

7 "Did You not, O our God, drive out the inhabitants of this land before Your people Israel and give it to the descendants of Abraham Your friend forever?

8 "They have lived in it, and have built You a sanctuary there for Your name, saying,

9 'Should evil come upon us, the sword, or judgment, or pestilence, or famine, we will stand before this house and before You (for Your name is in this house) and cry to You in our distress, and You will hear and deliver us.'

10 "Now behold, the sons of Ammon and Moab and Mount Seir, whom You did not let Israel invade when they came out of the land of Egypt (they turned aside from them and did not destroy them),

11 see how they are rewarding us by coming to drive us out from Your possession which You have given us as an inheritance.

12 "O our God, will You not judge them? For we are powerless before this great multitude who are coming against us; nor do we know what to do, but our eyes are on You."

• What did you learn from Jehoshaphat that you can apply to your own prayer life? *Fasting from things that distract from prayer. Call on God, the battle is His.*

OBSERVE

We saw that part of Jehoshaphat's prayer was devoted to reminding God of His promises and then asking for His deliverance. But first, like Jesus, he opened his prayer by honoring God and acknowledging who He is.

If we're going to follow Jesus' example by incorporating worship into our prayers and exalting God's name, we need to be familiar with who He is. The Bible uses numerous names for God, each of which reveals something about His character. Let's look at several Old Testament passages to consider three of God's names and to learn what they imply for our worship.[2]

First, let's go to Genesis 14. Abram, whose name was later changed to Abraham,

---

[2] For a more detailed study of the names of God, we recommend *Lord, I Want to Know You,* by Kay Arthur, published by WaterBrook Press.

had just returned from a battle where he defeated five kings and rescued his nephew Lot, along with several others.

Leader: *Read Genesis 14:18–20 aloud.*
- *Have the group say aloud and mark every reference to* **God Most High** *with a triangle.*

DISCUSS

- What name for God is used three times in this passage?

- What additional description of God is given in verse 19? *Possessor of Heaven + Earth*

INSIGHT

The term *God Most High* is the English equivalent of El-Elyon. It is a name that speaks of the sovereignty of God.

- What, exactly, had God done for Abram, according to Melchizedek? *10% gift. pre law.*

delivered him.

GENESIS 14:18–20

18 And Melchizedek king of Salem brought out bread and wine; now he was a priest of God Most High.△

19 He blessed him and said, "Blessed be Abram of God Most△ High, Possessor of heaven and earth;

20 and blessed be △ God Most High, Who has delivered your enemies into your hand." He gave him a tenth of all.

PSALM 91:1–9

1 He who dwells in the shelter of the Most High will abide in the shadow of the Almighty.

2 I will say to the LORD, "My refuge and my fortress, my God, in whom I trust!"

3 For it is He who delivers you from the snare of the trapper and from the deadly pestilence.

4 He will cover you with His pinions, and under His wings you may seek refuge; His faithfulness is a shield and bulwark.

5 You will not be afraid of the terror by night, or of the arrow that flies by day;

OBSERVE

Leader: *Read Psalm 91:1–9 aloud.*

• *Have the group say and mark every reference to **God**, including synonyms and pronouns, with a triangle.*

DISCUSS

• What name is used twice in this passage to describe God?

Most High

• What other descriptions of God did you notice?

▷ *Refuge, fortress, deliverer, shield, protector,*

• How would knowing these things about God help you in times of trouble?

helps you to trust

• Discuss how knowing God as the Most High relates to worship and how that might affect your prayer life.

Honor, Security.

OBSERVE

Leader: *Read Psalm 23:1–6 aloud.*

• *Have the group number **each action God takes** in this passage. (The first—"makes me lie down in green pastures"—is numbered for you.)*

6 of the pestilence
that stalks in darkness,
or of the destruction
that lays waste at noon.

7 A thousand may
fall at your side and
ten thousand at your
right hand, but it shall
not approach you.

8 You will only look
on with your eyes and
see the recompense of
the wicked.

9 For you have made
the LORD, my refuge,
even the Most High,
your dwelling place.

PSALM 23:1–6

1 The LORD is my
shepherd, I shall not
want.

2 He makes me lie
down in green pas-
tures; He leads me
beside quiet waters.

3 He restores my soul; He guides me in the paths of righteousness for His name's sake.

4 Even though I walk through the valley of the shadow of death, I fear no evil, for You are with me; Your rod and Your staff, they comfort me.

5 You prepare a table before me in the presence of my enemies; You have anointed my head with oil; my cup overflows.

6 Surely goodness and lovingkindness will follow me all the days of my life, and I will dwell in the house of the LORD forever.

DISCUSS

• What role does the psalmist attribute to the Lord in this passage?

Shepherd, host

• List God's actions on our behalf as described in Psalm 23 and numbered by you.

• In practical terms, how might we see evidence that God is acting in these particular ways in our own lives?

• How can knowing God as your shepherd impact your personal prayer life? your worship?

OBSERVE

Let's look at one more description or name of God.

Leader: *Read Exodus 15:26 and Psalm 107:17–21 aloud. Have the group say and…*
  - *mark with a triangle every reference to* **God,** *including pronouns and synonyms such as* **the Lord.**
  - *put an* **F** *over every reference to* **fools,** *including pronouns.*

DISCUSS

Who does God say He is in Exodus 15:26?

INSIGHT

The Hebrew name used to describe God as healer is *Jehovah Rapha,* which literally means "the Lord who heals."

- What did you learn from marking the references to *fools* in Psalm 107?

EXODUS 15:26

26 And He [God] △ said, "If you will give earnest heed to the voice of the L○RD your God, and do what is right in His sight, and give ear to His commandments, and keep all His statutes, I will put none of the diseases on you which I have put on the Egyptians; for I, the L○RD, am your healer."

PSALM 107:17–21

17 Fools, because of F their rebellious way, and because of their F iniquities, were afflicted.

18 Their soul abhorred all kinds of food, and they drew near to the F gates of death.

19 Then they cried out to the LORD in their trouble; He saved them out of their distresses.

20 He sent His word and healed them, and delivered them from their destructions.

21 Let them give thanks to the LORD for His lovingkindness, and for His wonders to the sons of men!

- Why did they cry out, or pray, to God?

- What action(s) did God take in response to their prayer?

- Discuss how understanding God's role as your healer might affect your prayers.

WRAP IT UP

In Matthew 6:5–15 Jesus gave us a model for prayer that includes several key elements, the first of which is worship: "Our Father who is in heaven, hallowed be Your name." Someone has defined worship as our response to the grace and mercy of God. We worship God by acknowledging who He is and how He acts on our behalf, which we learn by studying His character as revealed in His Word.

For example, the Bible reveals Him to be God Most High, completely in control of the circumstances of our lives. Nothing escapes His awareness; no circumstance is beyond His reach. He is able and willing to hear your prayer and answer you in your time of trouble. As your Shepherd and your Healer, God offers to restore your soul and save you out of your distresses.

Please note that when you look at prayers in the Bible, you never find God's faithful servants repeating the same word or phrase over and over such as "Praise You, Jesus; Praise You, Jesus." Instead the worshiper rehearses the character of God and His ways, reminding Him of His faithfulness and His wonderful promises. The pagans often worked themselves up through excited and frenzied repetition of a phrase in the worship of their gods. But not the children of God! Our worship is based not on emotion but on truth; not on the fervency of our words but on the faithfulness of God.

Leader: Close with a time of prayer. Invite the group to worship God by simply acknowledging who He is. You might suggest they use a phrase or a single word to describe in prayer who God is. Then close by reading Psalm 107:1–13:

> Oh give thanks to the LORD, for He is good,
>> For His lovingkindness is everlasting.
> Let the redeemed of the LORD say so,
>> Whom He has redeemed from the hand of the adversary
> And gathered from the lands,
>> From the east and from the west,
>> From the north and from the south.
> They wandered in the wilderness in a desert region;
>> They did not find a way to an inhabited city.
> They were hungry and thirsty;
>> Their soul fainted within them.
> Then they cried out to the LORD in their trouble;
>> He delivered them out of their distresses.
> He led them also by a straight way,
>> To go to an inhabited city.
> Let them give thanks to the LORD for His lovingkindness,
>> And for His wonders to the sons of men!
> For He has satisfied the thirsty soul,
>> And the hungry soul He has filled with what is good.
> There were those who dwelt in darkness and in the shadow of death,
>> Prisoners in misery and chains,
> Because they had rebelled against the words of God
>> And spurned the counsel of the Most High.

Therefore He humbled their heart with labor;

They stumbled and there was none to help.

Then they cried out to the LORD in their trouble;

He saved them out of their distresses.

This week we'll continue to study the first element of prayer by looking specifically at the role of thanksgiving in our worship.

As you draw near to God, as you cry out to Him, as you pray…do you ever find yourself simply thanking Him for what He has done in your life? And then, does God's grace and mercy move you beyond thanksgiving to swearing allegiance to Him? It certainly should, dear friend. And that's where our study this week will take us. We'll discover how our worship of God logically leads to undying loyalty to His kingdom.

You have an awesome study before you. Enjoy your time in God's Word.

OBSERVE

As a young man, the prophet Daniel was taken captive during a Babylonian siege of Jerusalem and assigned to be trained for service in the court of King Nebuchadnezzar. When the king dreamed a dream that no one could interpret, Daniel sought God for an answer. Let's look at what happened next.

Leader: Read aloud Daniel 2:19–23. Have the group say aloud and…

• *mark with a triangle every reference to* **God,** *including pronouns.*

• *double underline the word* **thanks.**

DANIEL 2:19–23

19 Then the mystery was revealed to Daniel in a night vision. Then Daniel blessed the God of heaven;

20 Daniel said, "Let the name of God be blessed forever and ever, for wisdom and power belong to Him.

21 "It is He who changes the times and the epochs; He removes kings and establishes kings; He gives wisdom to wise men and knowledge to men of understanding.

22 "It is He who reveals the profound and hidden things; He knows what is in the darkness, and the light dwells with Him.

23 "To You, O God of my fathers, I give thanks and praise, for You have given me wisdom and power; even now You have made known to me what we requested of You, for You have made known to us the king's matter."

DISCUSS

• What characteristics of God did Daniel highlight in these verses?

• Discuss how you see worship being manifested in this passage.

• Discuss any insights from Daniel's prayer that might relate to your personal prayer life.

OBSERVE

Leader: Read aloud the following passages from Philippians 4 and Psalms 100 and 118. Have the group…

- *draw a triangle over every reference to* **the Lord,** *including synonyms and pronouns.*
- *double underline the words* **thanks** *and* **thanksgiving.**
- *put a* **P** *over every reference to* **prayer** *and* **pray,** *including synonyms such as* **supplication, requests,** *and* **call upon.**

DISCUSS

- What did you learn about the Lord and our relationship to Him from these passages? What are we to do?

PHILIPPIANS 4:4–6

⁴ Rejoice in the Lord always; again I will say, rejoice!

⁵ Let your gentle spirit be known to all men. The Lord is near.

⁶ Be anxious for nothing, but in every-thing by prayer and supplication with thanksgiving let your requests be made known to God.

PSALM 100:1–4

¹ Shout joyfully to the LORD, all the earth.

² Serve the LORD with gladness; come before Him with joyful singing.

3 Know that the LORD Himself is God; it is He who has made us, and not we ourselves; we are His people and the sheep of His pasture.

4 Enter His gates with thanksgiving and His courts with praise. Give thanks to Him, bless His name.

PSALM 118:1–9

1 Give thanks to the LORD, for He is good; for His lovingkindness is everlasting.

2 Oh let Israel say, "His lovingkindness is everlasting."

3 Oh let the house of Aaron say, "His lovingkindness is everlasting."

• What did you learn about prayer from these verses?

• What relationship do you see between prayer and thanksgiving?

• According to Philippians 4:6, what is to accompany our prayers and requests? Discuss what that looks like in the life of a believer and how this element of prayer relates to you.

OBSERVE

We've seen that worship is the first and the last element of the model prayer, and thanksgiving is a natural part of worship. As we pray, we're to enter His gates with thanksgiving and His courts with praise.

The second element of prayer—our declaration of allegiance to the kingdom of God—is a natural result of worship and especially of thanksgiving. When we think about what He has done in our lives, the

4 Oh let those who fear the LORD say, "His lovingkindness is everlasting."

5 From my distress I called upon the LORD; the LORD answered me and set me in a large place.

6 The LORD is for me; I will not fear; what can man do to me?

7 The LORD is for me among those who help me; therefore I will look with satisfaction on those who hate me.

8 It is better to take refuge in the LORD than to trust in man.

9 It is better to take refuge in the LORD than to trust in princes.

PHILIPPIANS 3:20

20 For our citizenship is in heaven, from which also we eagerly wait for a Savior, the Lord Jesus Christ.

MATTHEW 6:33

33 "But seek first His kingdom and His righteousness, and all these things will be added to you."

only reasonable response is to pledge our undying loyalty to Him: "Your kingdom come. Your will be done, on earth as it is in heaven" (Matthew 6:10).

Leader: Read aloud Philippians 3:20 and Matthew 6:33.

• *Have the group say aloud and draw a cloud shape like this ⟨⟩ around the words* **citizenship** *and* **kingdom**.

DISCUSS

• As believers, where is our citizenship?

• According to Matthew 6:33, what is our responsibility as citizens of heaven?

• What evidence does your life give that you are fulfilling that responsibility?

• Take a moment and think about your typical day. How much time do you spend pursuing God's kingdom? What does this reveal about your real loyalties?

• What earthly entanglements tend to interfere with your loyalty to God, and how will you deal with them?

OBSERVE

Leader: Read 2 Timothy 2:15 and Matthew 4:4 aloud.

> • *Have the group say and put a **W** over each occurrence of **word.***

DISCUSS

• What did you learn from marking references to the Word of God in these verses? How would you describe its importance in the life of a believer?

• As a citizen of heaven what should your food be? What does the amount of time you spend with God's Word reveal about your allegiance? Explain your answer.

2 TIMOTHY 2:15

15 Be diligent to present yourself approved to God as a workman who does not need to be ashamed, accurately handling the word of truth.

MATTHEW 4:4

4 But He [Jesus] answered and said, "It is written, 'Man shall not live on bread alone, but on every word that proceeds out of the mouth of God.'"

MARK 8:34

34 And He [Jesus] summoned the crowd with His disciples, and said to them, "If anyone wishes to come after Me, he must deny himself, and take up his cross and follow Me."

OBSERVE

Leader: *Read aloud Mark 8:34.*

* *Have the group say and mark each pronoun referring to **Jesus** with a cross, like this:* ✝

DISCUSS

• When Jesus called men and women to follow Him, what kind of loyalty did He require?

• The cross was an instrument of death. Discuss what this tells you about following Jesus.

• You may be wondering at this point what these passages have to do with your prayer life. Stay with us through one more passage, and then we'll tie it all together. As you read, keep in mind the second part of the Lord's Prayer: "Your kingdom come. Your will be done, on earth as it is in heaven."

OBSERVE

In Matthew 7:18–27, Jesus described to His disciples what it means to be part of His kingdom.

Leader: Read Matthew 7:18–27 aloud. Have the group say and...

- *mark every reference to **Jesus** with a cross. Watch carefully for pronouns and synonyms, such as **Your name.***
- *draw a semicircle over every reference to **fruit**, like this:* ⌒
- *underline the phrases **does the will of My Father** and **hears these words of Mine.***

DISCUSS

- What did you learn by marking *fruit*?

MATTHEW 7:18–27

18 "A good tree cannot produce bad fruit, nor can a bad tree produce good fruit.

19 "Every tree that does not bear good fruit is cut down and thrown into the fire.

20 "So then, you will know them by their fruits.

21 "Not everyone who says to Me, 'Lord, Lord,' will enter the kingdom of heaven, but he who does the will of My Father who is in heaven will enter.

22 "Many will say to Me on that day, 'Lord, Lord, did we not prophesy in Your name, and in Your

name cast out demons, and in Your name perform many miracles?'

23 "And then I will declare to them, 'I never knew you; depart from Me, you who practice lawlessness.'

24 "Therefore everyone who hears these words of Mine and acts on them, may be compared to a wise man who built his house on the rock.

25 "And the rain fell, and the floods came, and the winds blew and slammed against that house; and yet it did not fall, for it had been founded on the rock.

26 "Everyone who hears these words of Mine and does not act

• What distinguishes real believers from imitators?

• What did you learn about Jesus from this passage?

• As you examine the context of the phrases *does the will of My Father* and *hears these words of Mine,* what truths do you find about being in a relationship with God?

• Is there any point in praying if you are unwilling to be loyal to God's kingdom by doing your part to accomplish His will? Explain your answer.

OBSERVE

What if you've done things that violate the will of God? What if you've been disloyal to the kingdom?

Leader: Read 1 John 1:9 aloud.
> • *Have the group say and mark with a triangle the pronoun **He**, which refers here to **God**.*

INSIGHT

Sin is a violation of God's law. *To confess* is to say the same thing about your sin that God says. In other words, it means to agree with God that what you have done is wrong.

To forgive means "to send away or dismiss." When we admit our sins, God dismisses them from us. He makes us clean.

---

on them, will be like a foolish man who built his house on the sand.

27 "The rain fell, and the floods came, and the winds blew and slammed against that house; and it fell—and great was its fall."

1 JOHN 1:9

9 If we confess our sins, He is faithful and righteous to forgive us our sins and to cleanse us from all unrighteousness.

DISCUSS

• What can you do if you have sinned against God? Discuss exactly what that means based on what you learned from the Insight Box.

• What two things will God do if we confess our sins?

• On what basis can we be certain He will do this? What compels Him to action?

WRAP IT UP

This week we saw that thanksgiving is a vital element of worship, the first element of the model prayer given to us by Jesus. Paul even commanded that we pray with thanksgiving. To be honest, being thankful in every circumstance requires faith. Sometimes life hurts, but faith says, "God is still on His throne." Faith believes God remains in control even when everything around us seems wrong. By contrast, if we question the authority and power of God, our prayer life will never be what it should be.

The second element of the Lord's Prayer is a declaration of allegiance, or loyalty, to God. As believers, we are citizens of heaven. Loyalty to the kingdom, submission to God's will, means we must die to ourselves and surrender completely to Him.

Have you ever heard someone say—or perhaps said yourself—"I know I should pray more, but…" or "I know I should study my Bible, but…" or "I know I should witness, but…" But what? The honest way to finish such sentences would be "but my first allegiance is not to God." When our first loyalty is to God's kingdom, we will invest our time in ways that reflect that loyalty.

Are you still holding out on God? Are you giving Him only part of your life while trying to retain control of the rest? Friend, your prayer life will never be effective, it will never be vibrant, and it will never be alive until you swear unconditional allegiance to the kingdom of God.

Leader: *If time permits, have the group spend time in prayer, inviting God to search their hearts and reveal anything that hinders them from an undivided allegiance to the hastening of the coming of His kingdom. Encourage them to examine themselves to see if they are truly in the kingdom.*

During the past three weeks we've been looking at what the Bible says about prayer and how we're to approach God. We've been using as our outline the Lord's Prayer, the model Jesus provided when the disciples asked Him to teach them how to pray.

As we've considered the first two elements in the Lord's Prayer—worship and declaration of allegiance—you may have been wondering, *When do we get to the part where we tell God what we need?* That's exactly what we'll be covering this week: petition and intercession.

But before we begin, may we ask you a question? Have you ever wondered if God still answers prayer? Secretly, deep in your soul, have you been afraid to ask Him for what you really need? Afraid He won't or can't come through? Friend, He can, He does. And we pray that our study this week will be an eye-opening experience, enabling you to see the *God who provides* in a fresh new way.

OBSERVE

In Matthew 6:11 Jesus prayed, "Give us this day our daily bread." This simple sentence demonstrates that prayer can and should involve presenting our requests to God. Let's look at some other verses that support this element of prayer.

Leader: *Read aloud Luke 11:1, 5–10. Have the group do the following:*

LUKE 11:1, 5–10

1 It happened that while Jesus was praying in a certain place, after He had finished, one of His disciples said to Him, "Lord, teach us to pray just as John also taught his disciples."

⁵ Then He said to them, "Suppose one of you has a friend, and goes to him at midnight and says to him, 'Friend, lend me three loaves;

⁶ for a friend of mine has come to me from a journey, and I have nothing to set before him';

⁷ and from inside he answers and says, 'Do not bother me; the door has already been shut and my children and I are in bed; I cannot get up and give you anything.'

⁸ "I tell you, even though he will not get up and give him anything because he is his friend, yet because of

- *Draw a squiggly line under each occurrence of the words **ask, asks, seek, seeks, knock, knocks:***
- *Put a **P** over the word **pray**, along with any synonyms.*
- *Underline the word **persistence.***

DISCUSS

- What did you learn about prayer from this passage?

- How persistent should we be? Explain your answer.

- What is the promise we have in this passage?

- What support do you find in this passage for the practice of intercession—praying on behalf of others?

• Are you asking? Are you seeking? Are you knocking? Or are you just sitting and hoping? What difference will your answer make?

Leader: Invite someone in the group to share an occasion from their personal experience in which they saw persistence in prayer elicit a response from God.

OBSERVE

Leader: Read aloud 1 John 5:14–15 and John 15:7.

> • *Have the group put a* **P** *over each occurrence of the words* **ask** *and* **requests.**

DISCUSS

• What connection, if any, can you find between these two passages?

• According to these verses, what is necessary for a prayer to be heard and answered?

his persistence he will get up and give him as much as he needs.

9 "So I say to you, ask, and it will be given to you; seek, and you will find; knock, and it will be opened to you.

10 "For everyone who asks, receives; and he who seeks, finds; and to him who knocks, it will be opened."

1 JOHN 5:14–15

14 This is the confidence which we have before Him, that, if we ask anything according to His will, He hears us.

15 And if we know that He hears us in whatever we ask, we know that we have the requests which we have asked from Him.

JOHN 15:7

7 "If you abide in Me, and My words abide in you, ask whatever you wish, and it will be done for you."

PHILIPPIANS 4:6

6 Be anxious for nothing, but in everything by prayer and supplication with thanksgiving let your requests be made known to God.

• If we fulfill these conditions, what should we expect?

• Are there any restrictions on what we can ask for? If so, what are they?

OBSERVE

Leader: Read aloud Philippians 4:6.

   • *Have the students mark the word **prayer** with a* **P.**

INSIGHT

By way of reminder, *supplication* means "to ask for favor, or mercy, or grace."

DISCUSS

• What, according to this passage, are we supposed to be anxious for?

• What is our alternative to being anxious?

• The Word here is plain: make your requests known to God. Are you worrying, nervous, anxious? Or are you asking? What difference will your answer make in your life and in your prayers?

OBSERVE

By now you've got the idea: *ask!*

But how do you know the will of God? How can you know for certain that what you are asking is in line with His will?

Leader: Read Romans 12:1–2 aloud. Have the group...
- *circle every occurrence of the words **you** and **your.***
- *double underline the word **will.***

DISCUSS

• What is our "spiritual service of worship"?

• Discuss what it means to present your body as a sacrifice.

ROMANS 12:1–2

1 Therefore I urge you, brethren, by the mercies of God, to present your bodies a living and holy sacrifice, acceptable to God, which is your spiritual service of worship.

2 And do not be conformed to this world, but be transformed by the renewing of your mind, so that you may prove what the will of God is, that which is good and acceptable and perfect.

• What does verse 2 challenge us to do? What would that look like in your daily living? Explain your answer.

• Finally, what connection do you see between these two responsibilities and knowing the will of God?

MICAH 6:8

8 He [God] has told you, O man, what is good; and what does the LORD require of you but to do justice, to love kindness, and to walk humbly with your God?

OBSERVE

Leader: *Read aloud Micah 6:8.*

• *Have the group say aloud and underline the phrase* **what does the Lord require.**

DISCUSS

• List the three things the Lord requires of us.

• How can we know this is true? Who has told us?

• According to this verse, what is God's will for your life?

• How might this knowledge help you intercede in prayer for someone else?

OBSERVE

Leader: Read Psalm 119:1–8 aloud. Have the group do the following:

- • *underline each occurrence of the phrase **how blessed are those.***
- • *put a **W** over the many synonyms in this passage that refer to God's Word, including **law of the Lord, testimonies, His ways, precepts, statutes, commandments, righteous judgments.***

DISCUSS

• Describe those who are blessed. Why are they blessed?

• Just in case you missed it, what is the relationship between the Word of God and being blessed?

PSALM 119:1–8

1 How blessed are those whose way is blameless, who walk in the law of the LORD.

2 How blessed are those who observe His testimonies, who seek Him with all their heart.

3 They also do no unrighteousness; they walk in His ways.

4 You have ordained Your precepts, that we should keep them diligently.

5 Oh that my ways may be established to keep Your statutes!

6 Then I shall not be ashamed when I look upon all Your commandments.

7 I shall give thanks to You with uprightness of heart, when I learn Your righteous judgments.

8 I shall keep Your statutes; do not forsake me utterly!

• We saw in Romans 12:1–2 that believers are responsible to present our bodies as living sacrifices and to be transformed by the renewing of our minds. Based on what you've read in these verses from Psalm 119, what role does God's Word play in helping us carry out those responsibilities?

OBSERVE

Our study has shown that God urges us to present our requests to Him and that He has promised to hear us when we ask anything according to His will. We've learned that we can know His will by knowing His Word. As we study His Word, His Word abides in us and we begin to really know how to pray.

But what about those times when you prayed but things didn't turn out like you asked? What about those times when someone was not healed, when a child continued to walk in rebellion, when you've prayed yet a loved one died?

Let's look at several possible reasons your prayers weren't answered as you expected.

Leader: Read 2 Corinthians 12:7–9 aloud. Have the group…

- *circle each occurrence of the pronouns* **me, myself, I,** *and* **you** *when they refer to* **the apostle Paul,** *who is speaking in this passage.*
- *mark with a* **P** *the word* **implore.**

DISCUSS

- According to this passage, what problem was Paul praying about?

- How often did the apostle pray about this problem?

- How did God respond to Paul's request? Why did He respond that way? Explain your answer.

2 CORINTHIANS 12:7–9

7 Because of the surpassing greatness of the revelations, for this reason, to keep me from exalting myself, there was given me a thorn in the flesh, a messenger of Satan to torment me—to keep me from exalting myself!

8 Concerning this I implored the Lord three times that it might leave me.

9 And He has said to me, "My grace is sufficient for you, for power is perfected in weakness." Most gladly, therefore, I will rather boast about my weaknesses, so that the power of Christ may dwell in me.

JAMES 4:1–4

¹ What is the source of quarrels and conflicts among you? Is not the source your pleasures that wage war in your members?

² You lust and do not have; so you commit murder. You are envious and cannot obtain; so you fight and quarrel. You do not have because you do not ask.

³ You ask and do not receive, because you ask with wrong motives, so that you may spend it on your pleasures.

⁴ You adulteresses, do you not know that friendship with the world is hostility toward God? Therefore

OBSERVE

James, the brother of Jesus, wrote a letter to the extended church in which he addressed several problems regarding their behavior.

Leader: Read aloud James 4:1–4. Have the group...

- *circle each occurrence of the words **you** and **your.***
- *mark with a **P** the word **ask.***

DISCUSS

- Describe the people James was correcting. What problems marked their lives?

- What was the root of those problems, according to this passage?

- Why did these people not have what they wanted or perhaps needed?

• Discuss the reasons their prayers were not answered.

OBSERVE

The following verse is directed to husbands, but it further illustrates the connection between our behavior and the effectiveness of our prayers.

Leader: Read aloud 1 Peter 3:7.
> • *Have the group say aloud and circle the words* you *and* your.

DISCUSS

• What would prevent a husband from having his prayers answered?

• Might this principle apply to anyone else? Explain your answer.

whoever wishes to be a friend of the world makes himself an enemy of God.

1 PETER 3:7

7 You husbands in the same way, live with your wives in an understanding way, as with someone weaker, since she is a woman; and show her honor as a fellow heir of the grace of life, so that your prayers will not be hindered.

WRAP IT UP

How do I pray? This has been man's question for at least two thousand years, as we know from the disciples' request of Jesus. This week we looked at the elements of intercession and petition. We read Jesus' promise that if we ask anything in accordance with His will, we will receive it. Does this statement make you nervous? Whatever we ask? Have you ever been afraid to ask aloud, afraid to put God on the spot? Have you worried that if He doesn't come through, He might look bad and it will be your fault? Don't worry. Ask.

Jack Arthur, the president and cofounder of Precept Ministries International, is a man who believes God still answers prayers—and lives that belief daily. His life includes example upon example of answered prayer.

Years ago, while serving with the Pocket New Testament League in Africa, Jack was driving from village to village, showing a film that explained the gospel in a common dialect. Deep in the heart of Zimbabwe, he had just received permission from a village chief to show the film when he heard a thunderstorm approaching and noticed the black clouds moving in quickly. Unwilling to let weather stop them from presenting the gospel, Jack and two other missionaries got on their knees beside the truck, and Jack prayed, "Lord, stop the rain, for Your glory." The rain stopped about two blocks from the clearing. The entire village heard about Jesus, and the results were amazing. When they finished talking to the people and drove away, the missionaries could see exactly where the storm had been held back. As if a line had been drawn across the road, one side remained dusty while mud puddles had collected on the other.

Jack Arthur still believes God answers prayer, and we've seen countless amazing results of his prayer life here at Precept Ministries International. Yet as amazing as it may seem, each of us has the potential to have a similarly vibrant prayer life. God doesn't answer Jack's prayers because He likes Jack better than anyone else. God answers Jack's prayers because Jack prays, because Jack believes God hears him, and because Jack knows the Father's will.

The closer you grow to your heavenly Father, the more intimately you will know His will, His ways, and His love for you. God is waiting to spend time with you. Talk to Him.

Leader: *Close by giving the students time to pray silently. Challenge them to ask God for something they need. It might be a financial need, a physical healing, seeing a rebellious loved one turn to God, or maybe peace in a trying time. Then encourage them to continue to ask each day this week. Next week invite them to share what has happened as they sought God and asked.*

In our study of prayer last week, we looked at the element of petition, including some possible reasons our requests are not granted. While Jesus has promised that the Father will respond when we ask anything in His name, we can't expect an answer when our requests aren't in line with the will of God or if our motivations are selfish. This week as we cover the last two elements of the Lord's Prayer—confession of sin and request for deliverance—we'll learn how our relationships with God and others impact the effectiveness of our prayers.

Some of this week's lesson will sound familiar, but it is worth the review to be sure we understand God's perspective.

OBSERVE

Immediately following His model prayer, Jesus offered further teaching on the element of confession in prayer.

Leader: Read aloud Matthew 6:12, 14–15.
- *Have the group say aloud and draw a box around every occurrence of the words forgive and forgiven:* ☐

DISCUSS

• Compare verses 12 and 14. In this context, what do you think Jesus meant by the word *debts* in verse 12? Explain your answer.

MATTHEW 6:12, 14–15

12 "'And forgive us our debts, as we also have forgiven our debtors.'

14 "For if you forgive others for their transgressions, your heavenly Father will also forgive you.

15 "But if you do not forgive others, then your Father will not forgive your transgressions."

• How does offending or being offended compare to a debt?

• Have you ever felt that someone "owed you" after having injured or offended you? Explain your answer.

• What two actions was Jesus modeling for us in verse 12?

• According to verses 14–15, what will be the result when we follow His example?

• Based on what you read in verse 15, discuss what happens when we refuse to forgive someone else.

MATTHEW 5:23–24

23 "Therefore if you are presenting your offering at the altar, and there remember that your brother has something against you,

OBSERVE

Just how seriously does God take our relationships with others? Let's find out.

Leader: *Read aloud Matthew 5:23–24. Have the group…*
  • *circle the words* ***you*** *and* ***your.***
  • *double underline each occurrence of the word* ***offering.***

INSIGHT

Presenting your offering at the altar represents the same idea as worshiping for us today.

DISCUSS

• What qualifications for worship did Jesus give in this passage?

• What connection do you find in these verses between your relationship with God and your relationship with others?

OBSERVE

Last week we learned that how a husband treats his wife affects his prayer life. But does the principle apply to other relationships?

Leader: *Read Romans 12:10, 14–19, 21. Have the group…*
   • *underline every phrase that refers to **the things we as believers are supposed to do.***

24 leave your offering there before the altar and go; first be reconciled to your brother, and then come and present your offering."

ROMANS 12:10, 14–19, 21

10 Be devoted to one another in brotherly love; give preference to one another in honor.

14 Bless those who persecute you; bless and do not curse.

15 Rejoice with those who rejoice, and weep with those who weep.

16 Be of the same mind toward one another; do not be haughty in mind, but associate with the lowly. Do not be wise in your own estimation.

17 Never pay back evil for evil to anyone. Respect what is right in the sight of all men.

18 If possible, so far as it depends on you, be at peace with all men.

19 Never take your own revenge, beloved, but leave room for the wrath of God, for it is written, "Vengeance is Mine, I will repay," says the Lord.

21 Do not be overcome by evil, but overcome evil with good.

• *circle each occurrence of the words* **never** *and* **do not,** *then put a slash through the circle, like this:* ⊘

DISCUSS

• What is the standard of conduct indicated for believers in this passage? What are the things we are to do?

• What are we *not* to do?

OBSERVE

We have seen that God takes seriously our relationships with others, including our forgiveness of them and our seeking forgiveness when we've caused offense. Failure to do one or the other can negatively affect our prayer life. Now let's see what impact our relationship with God has on our prayers.

Leader: *Read aloud Isaiah 59:1–2 and Psalm 66:18.*

• *Have the group say and mark a slash through the words* **iniquities, sins,** *and* **wickedness,** *like this:* /

DISCUSS

• What did you learn by marking the references to *iniquity*? How does sin affect our relationship with God?

• What effect does unconfessed sin have on our prayers?

• Consider the current state of your prayer life. What, if anything, is hindering your prayers?

Leader: *Give the group time to reflect on this question.*

ISAIAH 59:1–2

1 Behold, the LORD's hand is not so short that it cannot save; nor is His ear so dull that it cannot hear.

2 But your iniquities have made a separation between you and your God, and your sins have hidden His face from you so that He does not hear.

PSALM 66:18

18 If I regard wickedness in my heart, the Lord will not hear.

1 JOHN 1:9

⁹ If we confess our sins, He is faithful and righteous to forgive us our sins and to cleanse us from all unrighteousness. ,

OBSERVE

So we've seen that our sin toward God, our poor treatment of others, and our refusal to forgive others will prevent us from gaining an audience with God. When we harbor sin in our hearts, He will not listen to what we have to say. So how can we resolve this problem?

Leader: Read aloud 1 John 1:9. Have the group say and...
- *mark a slash through each occurrence of the word **sins,** as before.*
- *draw a box around the word **forgive.***

INSIGHT

To *confess our sins* means "to say the same thing about our violations of God's law and will as God says about them." In short it means to admit we were wrong.

DISCUSS

- When we confess our sins to God, what happens?

• If it is so simple, why do you think so many people don't seek God's forgiveness? Explain your answer.

• Have you ever tried to justify your actions even when deep down you knew you were wrong? Why not just ask God to forgive you?

OBSERVE

We've seen how crucial the element of confession is for those who want to pray effectively. Now let's look again at the last verse in Jesus' model prayer as we turn our attention to the final element: request for deliverance.

Leader: Read aloud Matthew 6:13.
  • *Have the group say aloud and mark the word **deliver** with an arrow, like this:* ↑

DISCUSS

• What was Jesus asking for in this verse?

MATTHEW 6:13

13 " 'And do not lead us into temptation, but deliver us from evil. [For Yours is the kingdom and the power and the glory forever. Amen.]' "

• What does this passage teach us about the reality of evil?

• What can we do to seek protection from evil and deliverance from temptation?

MATTHEW 26:41

41 "Keep watching and praying that you may not enter into temptation; the spirit is willing, but the flesh is weak."

1 CORINTHIANS 10:13

13 No temptation has overtaken you but such as is common to man; and God is faithful, who will not allow you to be tempted beyond what you are able, but with the temptation will provide the way of escape also, so that you will be able to endure it.

OBSERVE

Leader: Read Matthew 26:41 and 1 Corinthians 10:13.

> • *Have the group draw a squiggly line under each occurrence of the words **temptation** and **tempted:*** ‿‿‿

DISCUSS

• What did you learn from marking the references to *temptation?*

• Discuss how this information should affect your prayer life.

• What insight do these verses give you into how you might pray for others?

OBSERVE

John 17 contains Jesus' prayer for us as His disciples. The way Jesus intercedes for us should serve as an example for our own prayer life.

Leader: Read John 17:14–19 aloud. Have the group…
- *say and mark with a cross* ✝ *the pronouns **I**, **Me**, and **myself**, which refer to **Jesus.***
- *circle the words **them** and **they.***

DISCUSS

- This prayer occurred at the close of Jesus' life, just before His arrest and crucifixion. What might the timing of this prayer indicate about its importance?

- How did Jesus, in His last hours, intercede for us?

JOHN 17:14–19

14 "I have given them Your word; and the world has hated them, because they are not of the world, even as I am not of the world.

15 "I do not ask You to take them out of the world, but to keep them from the evil one.

16 "They are not of the world, even as I am not of the world.

17 "Sanctify them in the truth; Your word is truth.

18 "As You sent Me into the world, I also have sent them into the world.

19 "For their sakes I sanctify Myself, that they themselves also may be sanctified in truth."

• What guidelines do you see here that would affect our prayers for ourselves? our prayers for others?

• Discuss what this passage indicates about warfare in the life of a Christian. Is it real? What was Jesus' perspective and response?

WRAP IT UP

So we've seen this week in our study of confession that God takes the issue of forgiveness seriously—very seriously! We come to our Father to plead, to pray, to cry out on the basis of His forgiveness extended to us through Jesus. He wants us to extend that same forgiveness to others.

Sometimes you might be tempted to say, "But you don't know what they did to me! You don't know how bad they hurt me!" Aren't you glad God doesn't say that when we come to Him? What terror would it cause if suddenly we heard from heaven, *"No forgiveness today. I'll have nothing to do with you. You have no idea how badly you've hurt Me."*

Instead, He loves and forgives us—and expects us to treat others with the same compassion.

If your prayer life is dull, unexciting, or just dead, invite God to examine your heart and reveal any areas of unforgiveness.[3] In our experience, the Holy Spirit will be quick to show you if you ask. If there is anyone in your life whom you have not forgiven, then follow these simple steps:

1. Ask God to forgive you for not having already forgiven them.
2. In prayer, tell God you forgive them—and really mean it.
3. Ask God to change your heart toward the one who injured you.
4. Pray for that person until God removes the burden.

---

[3] If you or someone in your class is struggling with this issue, we recommend the 40-Minute Study *Forgiveness: Breaking the Power of the Past.*

In addition to confession, we looked at the element of deliverance in our prayers. In today's society, the concept of deliverance may seem a little odd, even eccentric. Even in many Christian circles, "Lord, deliver us from evil!" is rarely used in prayer. However, as you have seen, this is exactly what Jesus prayed for us: "Keep them from the evil one" (John 17:15).

Friend, the enemy is real. The enemy of your soul, Satan, hates you and has a terrible plan for your life. He is real and he is powerful. Our protection comes from knowing and crying out to the one true God, the creator of the heavens and the earth. Jesus understood this, and that is why He taught us to pray for protection.

Are you praying to the Lord of hosts, the commander of the armies of heaven, and asking Him to deliver you from evil? Does your prayer life include intercession for your spouse, your children, your parents, your friends, your church leadership—especially your pastor? We urge you to make the request for deliverance a regular part of your prayer: "Lord, deliver them from evil; protect them from the enemy."

Leader: *Guide your class in a time of prayer or give them time to pray silently. Afterward ask if anyone wants to share with the group something God has shown them during this week's session.*

In the past few weeks we've seen that prayer can be described as drawing near to God, and we've used the Lord's Prayer as our guide to the key elements of prayer. This week we're going to consider just a few of the countless passages in God's Word that give further insight on praying in accordance with God's will and in ways that draw us closer to His heart.

Leader: If time allows, discuss how each of these examples either follows the model of the Lord's Prayer or adds a new dimension to our understanding of prayer.

OBSERVE

Leader: Read aloud 2 Corinthians 1:20.

- *Have the group say aloud and draw a cloud shape like this ⟨☁⟩ around the word **promises.***

DISCUSS

- What did you learn about the promises of God in this verse?

- How will God respond to the promises He has made?

- Would it be effective to pray or even plead the promises of God? Why?

2 CORINTHIANS 1:20

20 For as many as are the promises of God, in Him they are yes; therefore also through Him is our Amen to the glory of God through us.

EXODUS 32:9–14

9 The LORD said to Moses, "I have seen this people, and behold, they are an obstinate people.

10 "Now then let Me alone, that My anger may burn against them and that I may destroy them; and I will make of you a great nation."

11 Then Moses entreated the LORD his God, and said, "O LORD, why does Your anger burn against Your people whom You have brought out from the land of Egypt with great power and with a mighty hand?

12 "Why should the Egyptians speak, saying, 'With evil intent

OBSERVE

As we consider the role of God's promises in our prayer life, let's look together at a conversation between Moses and God. This interaction took place soon after the Israelites left Egypt. In spite of having seen God's miracles and having experienced His mercy, they repeatedly sinned against God and tested Him at almost every turn.

Leader: Read Exodus 32:9–14 aloud. Have the group…
- *put a **P** over the word **entreated.***
- *draw a cloud around the word **swore.***

Leader: Read Exodus 32:9–14 again.
- *This time underline each **request** Moses made of God.*

DISCUSS

- What did God tell Moses He intended to do with the Israelites He'd brought out of Egypt, and why? *destroy them*

• What did God offer to do for Moses in verse 10? *Make a great nation out of Moses.*

• How would you have responded to God? *Whah!?*

• Describe Moses' response. On what did he base his request? *Interceeds for his people.*

• In verse 12, what concern did Moses raise? *[History] God's reputation*

• What did Moses remind God about in verse 13? *Covenent promise.*

• Did Moses' entreaty succeed?

He brought them out to kill them in the mountains and to destroy them from the face of the earth'? Turn from Your burning anger and change Your mind about doing harm to Your people.

13 "Remember Abraham, Isaac, and Israel, Your servants to whom You swore by Yourself, and said to them, 'I will multiply your descendants as the stars of the heavens, and all this land of which I have spoken I will give to your descendants, and they shall inherit it forever.'"

14 So the LORD changed His mind about the harm which He said He would do to His people.

GENESIS 18:22–33

22 Then the men turned away from there and went toward Sodom, while Abraham was still standing before the LORD.

23 Abraham came near and said, "Will You indeed sweep away the righteous with the wicked?

24 "Suppose there are fifty righteous within the city; will You indeed sweep it away and not spare the place for the sake of the fifty righteous who are in it?

25 "Far be it from You to do such a thing, to slay the righteous with the wicked, so that the righteous and the wicked are treated alike. Far be it

OBSERVE

Moses, as we've seen, interceded in prayer on behalf of his people, making his requests on the basis of God's character and promises. Let's look at another example of intercession. Watch as Abraham pleads with God on behalf of the citizens of Sodom and Gomorrah, among whom live Abraham's nephew, Lot, and his family.

Leader: Read Genesis 18:22–33 aloud. Have the group do the following:
- *Mark every reference to **the Lord,** including pronouns and synonyms, with a triangle: △*
- *Draw a box around each occurrence of the phrase **will You.***
- *Draw a box around each occurrence of the phrase **I will not,** then mark a slash through it, like this: ▱*

DISCUSS

• What principles did you learn from Abraham's intercession?

• According to verse 25, what was the basis for Abraham's intercession, and what does this reveal about his relationship with God?

God's Justice

He knows God.

from You! Shall not the Judge of all the earth deal justly?"

26 So the LORD said, "If I find in Sodom fifty righteous within the city, then I will spare the whole place on their account."

27 And Abraham replied, "Now behold, I have ventured to speak to the Lord, although I am but dust and ashes.

28 "Suppose the fifty righteous are lacking five, will You destroy the whole city because of five?" And He said, "I will not destroy it if I find forty-five there."

29 He spoke to Him yet again and said, "Suppose forty are found there?" And He said, "I will not do it on account of the forty."

30 Then he said, "Oh may the Lord not be angry, and I shall speak; suppose thirty are found there?" And He said, "I will not do it if I find thirty there."

31 And he said, "Now behold, I have ventured to speak to the Lord; suppose twenty are found there?" And He said, "I will not destroy it on account of the twenty."

32 Then he said, "Oh may the Lord not be angry, and I shall speak only this once; suppose ten are found there?" And He said, "I will not destroy it on account of the ten."

• What did you learn from Abraham's conversation with God that you can apply to your own prayer life?

Keep asking

OBSERVE

Let's see what we can learn about effective prayer from another hero of the Old Testament, Nehemiah. We'll look at how he sought God's help as he prepared to approach the king of Persia to ask for permission to rebuild the walls of Jerusalem.

Leader: Read Nehemiah 1:5–11 aloud. Have the group do the following:
- *Mark every reference to **God**, including pronouns and synonyms, with a triangle, as before.*
- *Put a **P** over every reference to **prayer**, including synonyms such as **beseech**.*
- *Draw a cloud over the word **remember**.*

DISCUSS

- What character qualities of God did Nehemiah call upon in this prayer?

lovingkindness.

33 As soon as He had finished speaking to Abraham the LORD departed, and Abraham returned to his place.

NEHEMIAH 1:5–11

5 I said, "I beseech You, O LORD God of heaven, the great and awesome God, who preserves the covenant and lovingkindness for those who love Him and keep His commandments,

6 let Your ear now be attentive and Your eyes open to hear the prayer of Your servant which I am praying before You now, day and night, on behalf of the sons of Israel Your servants, confessing the sins of the sons of Israel which

we have sinned against You; I and my father's house have sinned.

7 "We have acted very corruptly against You and have not kept the commandments, nor the statutes, nor the ordinances which You commanded Your servant Moses.

8 "Remember the word which You commanded Your servant Moses, saying, 'If you are unfaithful I will scatter you among the peoples;

9 but if you return to Me and keep My commandments and do them, though those of you who have been scattered were in the most remote part of the heavens, I will

• What promises did Nehemiah call on God to remember and fulfill?

• What principles or insights did you find in this passage that you can apply to your own prayer life?

Interceeds +
confesses sins of group.
—through family

gather them from there and will bring them to the place where I have chosen to cause My name to dwell.'

10 "They are _Your_ servants and _Your_ people whom You redeemed by _Your_ great power and by _Your_ strong hand.

11 "O Lord, I beseech You, may Your ear be attentive to the prayer of Your servant and the prayer of Your servants who delight to revere Your name, and make Your servant successful today and grant him compassion before this man." Now I was the cupbearer to the king.

DANIEL 9:4–6, 15–19

⁴ I prayed to the LORD my God and confessed and said, "Alas, O Lord, the great and awesome God, who keeps His covenant and lovingkindness for those who love Him and keep His commandments,

⁵ we have sinned, committed iniquity, acted wickedly and rebelled, even turning aside from Your commandments and ordinances.

⁶ "Moreover, we have not listened to Your servants the prophets, who spoke in Your name to our kings, our princes, our fathers and all the people of the land.

OBSERVE

Let's consider one more Old Testament example of prayer. In the following passage, listen as Daniel pleads with God to conclude His judgment on the people of Jerusalem for their unfaithfulness.

Leader: Read aloud Daniel 9:4–6, 15–19. Have the group mark...

- *every reference to* **the Lord,** *including pronouns and synonyms, with a triangle.*
- *every reference to* **prayer,** *including synonyms such as* **supplication,** *with a* **P.**

DISCUSS

- What character qualities of God did Daniel point out in this prayer?

lovingkindness,
forgiving,

• What promises did Daniel call on God to remember and fulfill?

Covenent w/ egypt

• According to verse 18, on what basis did <u>what basis did</u> Daniel make his request?

God's reputation

15 "And now, O Lord our God, who have brought Your people out of the land of Egypt with a mighty hand and have made a name for Yourself, as it is this day—we have sinned, we have been wicked.

16 "O Lord, in accordance with all Your righteous acts, let now Your anger and Your wrath turn away from Your city Jerusalem, Your holy mountain; for because of our sins and the iniquities of our fathers, Jerusalem and Your people have become a reproach to all those around us.

17 "So now, our God, listen to the prayer of Your servant and to his

supplications, and for Your sake, O Lord, let Your face shine on Your desolate sanctuary.

18 "O my God, incline Your ear and hear! Open Your eyes and see our desolations and the city which is called by Your name; for we are not presenting our supplications before You on account of any merits of our own, but on account of Your great compassion.

19 "O Lord, hear! O Lord, forgive! O Lord, listen and take action! For Your own sake, O my God, do not delay, because Your city and Your people are called by Your name."

• What did you learn from this passage that you can apply to your own prayer life?

> Prayer is effective.
> Intercede for others.
> Appeal to God's character and his promises.
> Request out of the basis of his Glory: Appeal to his Reputation.

OBSERVE

The passages we've just examined show us the bold prayers of men who knew the promises and the character of God. Remember, we have already seen that abiding in the Word gives us an understanding of the will of God. These men abided with God and in the Word of God until they knew the character of God, the promises of God, and therefore the will of God. Did you notice that they prayed not only for themselves but also interceded with God on behalf of those around them? We find similar concerns reflected in the words of the apostle Paul.

Leader: *Read aloud Ephesians 1:15–19.*
Have the group…
- *circle each occurrence of the words* **you** *and* **your.**
- *mark with a* **P** *the words* **prayers** *and* **pray.**

DISCUSS

- Specifically, line by line, what did Paul pray for these people?

- give thanks
- wisdom + Rev. to know God better.
- enlightened, know hope open heart to experience
- his power for us.

- What indications do you find that this prayer is within the will of God?

EPHESIANS 1:15–19

15 For this reason I too, having heard of the faith in the Lord Jesus which exists among you and your love for all the saints,

16 do not cease giving thanks for you, while making mention of you in my prayers;

17 that the God of our Lord Jesus Christ, the Father of glory, may give to you a spirit of wisdom and of revelation in the knowledge of Him.

18 I pray that the eyes of your heart may be enlightened, so that you will know what is the hope of His calling, what are the riches of the glory of His inheritance in the saints,

19 and what is the surpassing greatness of His power toward us who believe. These are in accordance with the working of the strength of His might.

EPHESIANS 3:14–21

14 For this reason I bow my knees before the Father,

15 from whom every family in heaven and on earth derives its name,

16 that He would grant you, according to the riches of His glory, to be strengthened with power through His Spirit in the inner man,

17 so that Christ may dwell in your hearts through faith; and that

• How could this prayer serve as our model in praying for others? for ourselves?

OBSERVE

Leader: Read aloud Ephesians 3:14–21. Have the group…

• *mark with a* **P** *the phrase* ***bow my knees.***

• *circle each occurrence of the words* ***you*** *and* ***your.***

• *mark with a triangle every reference to* ***God,*** *including synonyms such as* ***the Father*** *and pronouns such as* ***whom, He, His,*** *and* ***Him.***

DISCUSS

• Specifically, line by line, what did Paul pray for these people?

• What indications do you find that this prayer is within the will of God?

you, being rooted and grounded in love,

18 may be able to comprehend with all the saints what is the breadth and length and height and depth,

19 and to know the love of Christ which surpasses knowledge, that you may be filled up to all the fullness of God.

• How could this prayer serve as our model in praying for others? for ourselves?

20 Now to Him who is able to do far more abundantly beyond all that we ask or think, according to the power **H.S.** that works within us,

21 to Him be the glory in the church and in Christ Jesus to all generations forever and ever. Amen.

you've already given your all for me.

COLOSSIANS 1:9–12

⁹ For this reason also, since the day we heard of it, we have not ceased to pray for you and to ask that you may be filled with the knowledge of His will in all spiritual wisdom and understanding,

¹⁰ so that you will walk in a manner worthy of the Lord, to please Him in all respects, bearing fruit in every good work and increasing in the knowledge of God;

¹¹ strengthened with all power, according to His glorious might, for the attaining of all steadfastness and patience; joyously

OBSERVE

As our study comes to a close, let's quickly examine one more passage that provides a model for our personal prayer life.

Leader: Read aloud Colossians 1:9–12. Have the group...
- *mark the word **pray** with a **P.***
- *circle each occurrence of the word **you.***

DISCUSS

- Specifically, line by line, what did Paul pray for these people?

- What indications do you find that this prayer is within the will of God?

• How could this prayer serve as our model in praying for others? for ourselves?

12 giving thanks to the Father, who has qualified us to share in the inheritance of the saints in Light.

WRAP IT UP

We've examined prayer from many angles to answer the questions of what prayer is and how we're to pray if we truly want God to hear us. Only one question remains: *Do you pray?*

Prayer is the most normal activity of a child of God. Regardless of denomination or church affiliation, we hold this in common—yet few of us have truly made prayer a priority. *Do you pray?*

By prayer the sick have been healed, the wicked have been converted. By prayer the hurting are comforted, the depressed are encouraged, the confused see clearly. *Do you pray?*

Sometimes we wonder where our lives are headed. Sometimes we wish things were different. Instead of wondering and wishing, *why don't we pray?*

God moves when we ask, but it seems He often chooses not to move until we ask. Whatever decision you're facing, whatever worry weighs on your heart, all you need to do is draw near to God, cry out to Him. *Will you pray?*

In the following pages you'll find prayers taken from Scripture and formatted to make them easy to use in praying for yourself and interceding for others. Please use them. God invites you to draw near. *Will you pray?*

The LORD bless you, and keep you;
The LORD make His face shine on you, and be gracious to you;
The LORD lift up His countenance on you, and give you peace.
NUMBERS 6:24–26

Ephesians 1:17–19

Father, I pray that you would give _____ a spirit of wisdom and of revelation in the knowledge of You, open the eyes of their heart, that they will know what is the hope to which You have called them, what are the riches of Your glorious inheritance in the saints, and what is the immeasurable greatness of Your power toward us who believe, according to the working of Your great might.

Ephesians 3:16–19

Father, I am asking that according to the riches of Your glory, You will grant _____ to be strengthened with power through Your Spirit in their inner being, so that Christ may dwell in _____'s heart through faith—that _____, being rooted and grounded in love, may have strength to comprehend with all the saints what is the breadth and length and height and depth, and to know the love of Christ that surpasses knowledge, that they may be filled with all the fullness of God.

Colossians 1:9–12

Father, I ask that _____ will be filled with the knowledge of Your will in all spiritual wisdom and understanding, so as to walk in a manner worthy of You, fully pleasing to You, bearing fruit in every good work and increasing in the knowledge of You. May _____ be strengthened with all power, according to Your glorious might, for all endurance and patience with joy, giving thanks to the You, because You have qualified us to share in the inheritance of the saints in light.

Philippians 1:9–11

This I pray, that _____'s love may abound still more and more in real knowledge and all discernment, so that _____ may approve the things that are excellent, in order to be sincere and blameless until the day of Christ; having been filled with the fruit of righteousness which comes through Jesus Christ, to the glory and praise of God.

2 Thessalonians 1:11–12

To this end also I pray for _____ always, that our God will count _____ worthy of their calling, and fulfill every desire for goodness and the work of faith with power, so that the name of our Lord Jesus will be glorified in _____, and _____ in Him, according to the grace of our God and the Lord Jesus Christ.

2 Thessalonians 2:16–17

Now may our Lord Jesus Christ Himself and God our Father, who has loved us and given us eternal comfort and good hope by grace, comfort and strengthen _____ 's heart in every good work and word.

2 Thessalonians 3:1–2

Finally, Father, I pray that the word of the Lord will spread rapidly and be glorified, just as it did also with the early church; and that we will be rescued from perverse and evil men; for not all have faith.

40
MINUTE
BIBLE
STUDIES

No-Homework
That Help You

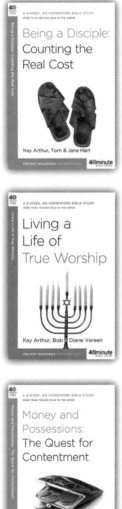

A 6-WEEK, NO-HOMEWORK BIBLE STUDY
MORE THAN 700,000 SOLD IN THE SERIES

Being a Disciple:
Counting the
Real Cost

Kay Arthur, Tom & Jane Hart

PRECEPT MINISTRIES INTERNATIONAL   40minute
BIBLE STUDY

A 6-WEEK, NO-HOMEWORK BIBLE STUDY
MORE THAN 700,000 SOLD IN THE SERIES

Having a Real
Relationship
with God

Kay Arthur

PRECEPT MINISTRIES INTERNATIONAL   40minute
BIBLE STUDY

A 6-WEEK, NO-HOMEWORK BIBLE STUDY
MORE THAN 700,000 SOLD IN THE SERIES

How Do You
Walk the Walk
You Talk?

Kay Arthur

PRECEPT MINISTRIES INTERNATIONAL   40minute
BIBLE STUDY

A 6-WEEK, NO-HOMEWORK BIBLE STUDY
MORE THAN 700,000 SOLD IN THE SERIES

Living a
Life of
True Worship

Kay Arthur, Bob & Diane Vereen

PRECEPT MINISTRIES INTERNATIONAL   40minute
BIBLE STUDY

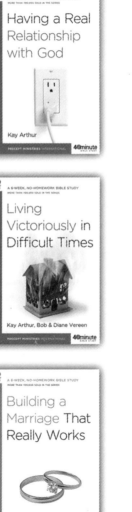

A 6-WEEK, NO-HOMEWORK BIBLE STUDY
MORE THAN 700,000 SOLD IN THE SERIES

Living
Victoriously in
Difficult Times

Kay Arthur, Bob & Diane Vereen

PRECEPT MINISTRIES INTERNATIONAL   40minute
BIBLE STUDY

A 6-WEEK, NO-HOMEWORK BIBLE STUDY
MORE THAN 700,000 SOLD IN THE SERIES

How to Make
Choices You
Won't Regret

Kay Arthur, David & BJ Lawson

PRECEPT MINISTRIES INTERNATIONAL   40minute
BIBLE STUDY

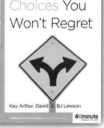

A 6-WEEK, NO-HOMEWORK BIBLE STUDY
MORE THAN 700,000 SOLD IN THE SERIES

Money and
Possessions:
The Quest for
Contentment

Kay Arthur & David Arthur

PRECEPT MINISTRIES INTERNATIONAL   40minute
BIBLE STUDY

A 6-WEEK, NO-HOMEWORK BIBLE STUDY
MORE THAN 700,000 SOLD IN THE SERIES

Building a
Marriage That
Really Works

Kay Arthur, David & BJ Lawson

PRECEPT MINISTRIES INTERNATIONAL   40minute
BIBLE STUDY

A 6-WEEK, NO-HOMEWORK BIBLE STUDY
MORE THAN 700,000 SOLD IN THE SERIES

How Do You
Know God's
Your Father?

Kay Arthur, David & BJ Lawson

PRECEPT MINISTRIES INTERNATIONAL   40minute
BIBLE STUDY

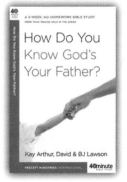

Bible Studies
Discover Truth For Yourself

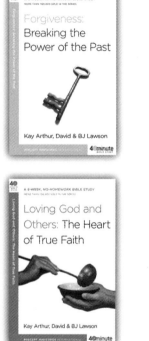

Also Available:

A Man's Strategy for Conquering Temptation
Rising to the Call of Leadership
Key Principles of Biblical Fasting
What Does the Bible Say About Sex?
Turning Your Heart Toward God
Fatal Distractions: Conquering Destructive Temptations
Spiritual Warfare: Overcoming the Enemy
The Power of Knowing God
Breaking Free from Fear

Another powerful study series from beloved Bible teacher

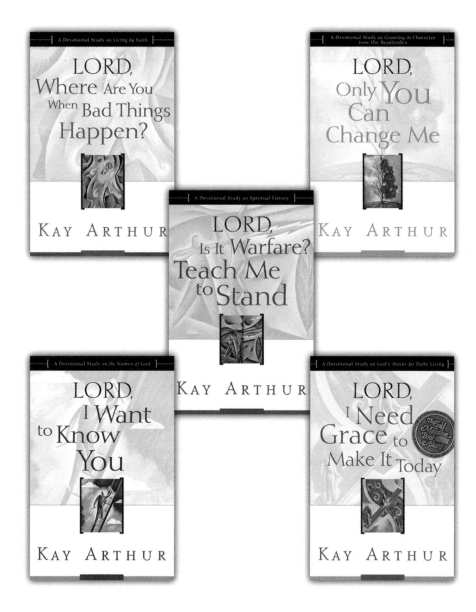

{ A Devotional Study on Living by Faith }

LORD,
Where Are You
When Bad Things
Happen?

KAY ARTHUR

{ A Devotional Study on Growing in Character from the Beatitudes }

LORD,
Only You
Can
Change Me

KAY ARTHUR

{ A Devotional Study on Spiritual Victory }

LORD,
Is It Warfare?
Teach Me
to Stand

KAY ARTHUR

{ A Devotional Study on the Names of God }

LORD,
I Want
to Know
You

KAY ARTHUR

{ A Devotional Study on God's Power for Daily Living }

LORD,
I Need
Grace to
Make It Today

KAY ARTHUR

KAY ARTHUR

The Lord series provides insightful, warm-hearted Bible studies designed to meet you where you are —and help you discover God's answers to your deepest needs.

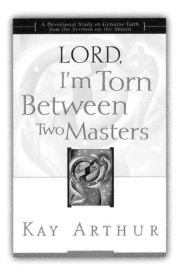

[A Devotional Study on Genuine Faith from the Sermon on the Mount]

LORD, I'm Torn Between Two Masters

KAY ARTHUR

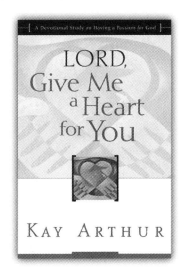

[A Devotional Study on Having a Passion for God]

LORD, Give Me a Heart for You

KAY ARTHUR

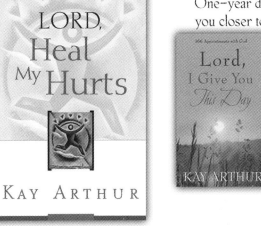

[A Devotional Study on God's Care and Deliverance]

LORD, Heal My Hurts

KAY ARTHUR

ALSO AVAILABLE:
One-year devotionals to draw you closer to the heart of God.

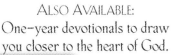

Lord, I Give You This Day

KAY ARTHUR

SEARCH MY HEART, O GOD

KAY ARTHUR

ABOUT THE AUTHORS AND PRECEPT MINISTRIES INTERNATIONAL

KAY ARTHUR is known around the world as an international Bible teacher, author, conference speaker, and host of the national radio and television programs *Precepts for Life,* which reaches a worldwide viewing audience of over 94 million. A four-time Gold Medallion Award–winning author, Kay has authored more than 100 books and Bible studies.

Kay and her husband, Jack, founded Precept Ministries International in 1970 in Chattanooga, Tennessee, with a vision to establish people in God's Word. Today, the ministry has a worldwide outreach. In addition to inductive study training workshops and thousands of small-group studies across America, PMI reaches nearly 150 countries with inductive Bible studies translated into nearly 70 languages, teaching people to discover Truth for themselves.

DAVID AND BJ LAWSON have been involved with Precept Ministries International since 1980. After nine years in the pastorate, they joined PMI full-time as directors of the student ministries and staff teachers and trainers. A featured speaker at PMI conferences and in Precept Upon Precept videos, David writes for the Precept Upon Precept series, the New Inductive Study Series, and the 40-Minute Bible Studies series. BJ has written numerous 40-Minute Bible Studies and serves as the chief editor and developer of the series. In addition she is a featured speaker at PMI women's conferences.

Contact Precept Ministries International for more information about inductive Bible studies in your area.

Precept Ministries International
P.O. Box 182218
Chattanooga, TN 37422-7218
800-763-8280
www.precept.org